Chromecast

A Step by Step User Guide for Beginners

Disclaimer

What This Book Has For You

This book will highlight the importance of the device that was introduced by Google for as low as $35 in detail. Chromecast by Google, which was introduced in July 2013, has proven to be big competition to Apple TV despite its small size.

While it's compared to Apple TV as well as Roku 3, the tiny device is really very unique, with useful features and its own set of limitations.

That being said, if you already have your hands on this device, this book will give you all the details to make the most out of this little magic you have in your hand. This book will help you maximize the usage and potential of Chromecast and if you haven't yet purchased the device, will encourage you to enjoy the unique experience the device brings along.

With all the details you require and all that you need to learn about this new hype, this book is just right for you.

This book offers you:

> Step by step details about Chromecast
> Easy-to-understand-and-implement details to help beginners get started
> Highlights on the advantages Google Chromecast

So read on and learn why Google Chromecast is the next 'hot device' to own!

Contents

All You Need to Know About Chromecast

Developed by Google, Chromecast is the latest digital media player that comes in a small package.

The HDMI dongle that isn't larger than 72mm, is capable of playing video/audio content through direct streaming on a modern HD TV using local internet Wi-Fi through.

You can select the media to play from web apps and mobile apps eligible for Chromecast. Users can also do it using a beta feature known as 'tab casting', which can emulate most content from the Google Chrome web browser.

The device that was introduced by Google on the 24th July 2013 was available on the very same day within the United States.

With price as low as $35, this tech-smart device soon became a hot device for people to own. It gained its initial popularity due to the limited-time offer it was introduced with – three months of free Netflix subscription.

This isn't all. This magical device has much more that brings it next to Apple TV and Roku 3. So read on and learn everything about this fantastic device called Chromecast by Google Chrome.

Steps in Setting up Your Device

This 2 inch dongle can be attached to your modern TV so you control and stream video from Netflix and YouTube using your laptop, tablet or smart phone.

You can simply connect the device using your local home internet through Wi-Fi. Then with the help of your laptop or your phone (iOS and Android), you can chose a video on Netflix or YouTube and directly stream it using the device and watch it on the TV. Don't forget to hit the 'cast' button to get started.

If you are the fortunate one to get your hands on this device before they were sold out, then you shouldn't waste time in learning how to make the most out of it. To get started, let's go through the steps of setting up your device first.

Make things convenient and enjoyable than ever before. Here's a detailed guide to help you set up your Google Chromecast device. Follow thoroughly and get started now.

Plugging Chromecast Device into Your Modern Television

1. Plugging in the device into your TV is the easiest part of the entire process. Don't worry if inserting the dongle physically is difficult due to the tricky placement of HDMI port in most televisions, you have the supplied HDMI extension that comes along with the device.

   Of course, you will also need to supply power to the Chromecast. To do so, plug in the micro USB adapter/cable.

   This process is pretty straightforward.

2. Next, connect the microUSB port in the device to the USB cable and the other end of the cable to the power adapter. Simply plug the power adapter into an outlet.

   The USB port can also be used with your Samsung Series 8000 HDTV to supply power to the device.

   Even if you have a different TV but there is a USB port available, don't forget to give it a try for the power.

   It is always more efficient to eliminate the clutter as much as possible.

3. Make sure you switch your TV's input to the right HDMI port.

   That's the right way to check if your Chromecast is connected and working perfectly fine if you see the screen above on your television.

Setting up Chromecast Utility

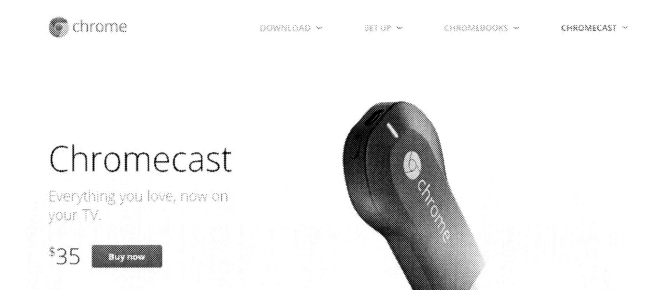

Use your Wi-Fi network to connect with your device.

If you don't already have one, install Google Chrome browser on your PC or Mac. It is important to remember that Chromecast will only work with Chrome browser.

To download the Google Chromecast utility, go to www.google.com/chromecast and click on the setup to download. It will take 3.5mb file space on Mac.

Using the Chromecast Utility

1. First of all, you must launch the utility for Chromecast you just downloaded. The moment you launch, it will start searching for the Google Chromecast device. When the device will be detected, it will display the name of the device both on your PC/Mac and TV. Click 'continue' to proceed with the installation.

2. Once the device connects, it will show a code on your PC as well as your TV.

3. You will see a button saying 'That's my code'. Click on that button if the code on the TV and the PC are same. By doing so, you will temporarily lose the internet connection. This is because the utility is making a secure connection with the Chromecast through Wi-Fi as well as configuring the Wi-Fi of the device to directly connect to your wireless network.

4. Next, you will have to choose your wireless internet connect. As mentioned earlier, the Google's Chromecast device is designed to directly stream audios and videos using the wireless internet network, it will need to connect to your Wi-Fi service.

    While using the Utility for Chromecast, choose your Wi-Fi network that you want to use, enter your password and connect with the internet immediately. If you want to change the name of your Chromecast device, now is the time to do so.

5. When the Chromecast is connected, you will see an image on your TV screen. The backgrounds may change with time to make user interface more interesting. You will also be given a signal, 'ready to cast' on your TV screen and the Chromecast utility will access the Chrome browser automatically to take you through a video tour that will guide you on using Chromecast.

Video Casting from PC

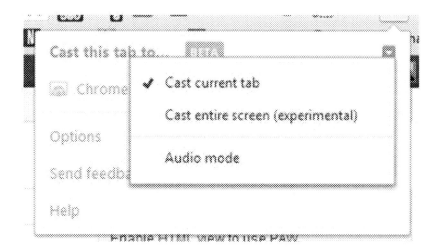

Time for entertainment. Open any video you like on Netflix or YouTube in the Chrome browser. You will see a small Chromecast icon appear on the right lower corner of the screen. As soon as you will click that icon, the video will start playing on your TV.

In order to cast a tab, click on the Chromecast icon that appears on the right upper corner of the screen (Chrome browser) and choose your device where you can read 'Cast this tab to…"

To discontinue casting a tab, access the same menu again and click on 'Stop Casting' to stop the process immediately.

Video Casting from Tablet or Phone (iOS and Android)

Chromecast can be used with Google Play Music, Google Play Movies, YouTube and Netflix applications on iOS and android. This restricts you from Tab Casting from a chrome browser using a mobile or tab.

Also note that Chromecast is compatible with tablets and smart phones that are running Android 2.3 and higher, and iOS 6 and higher.

Use your local internet Wi-Fi connection to connect your table or smartphone with Chromecast.

Access the application you wish to use (use applications that are compatible with Chromecast). When your device will recognize the Chromecast it will immediately show you a small Chromecast icon on the top right corner of the video you are playing. Click on this tiny icon and you will see a window popping up asking you to choose a screen on which you wish to see the video appear.

Bottom Line

That's all that you need to know about setting up Google Chromecast. Indeed, a gadget that costs as low as $35 dollars comes with lots of potential.

Simple Way to Cast Using Chromecast Applications

Casting to your television is an easy procedure. You can use your tablet or phone as a remote control for your television. To control your TV with your smartphone, laptop or tablet, open up an app supported by Chromecast. These are also referred as Chromecast apps.

You will find the Cast Button available on such apps. Once your device is connected with your TV, the Cast Button will automatically change to blue. This is a signal that you are now connected. Once the button turns blue, you can cast TV shows, movies and videos directly to your TV, using your phone, tablet or laptop as your remote control.

The following is a list of supported websites and applications that you can use:

YouTube.com and YouTube application
Google Play Movies and TV
Netflix.com and Netflix application
Hulu Plus

Google Play Music

HBOGo

Pandora

Red Bull.TV

Vevo

Songza

BeyondPod

aVia

Revisions3

RealPlayer Cloud

Viki

Plex

PostTV by the Washingtom Post

This is not all. The good news is that with the popularity of this tiny gadget, more and more apps are built to make Chromecast user interface friendly and convenient to use.

Making the Most out of Google Chrome Tabs and Online Videos

Chromecast is all about unexpected discoveries. Read on to find out how to make the most out of tabs and online videos using Google Chromecast.

Chromecast Device and Casting Web Pages Using Chrome

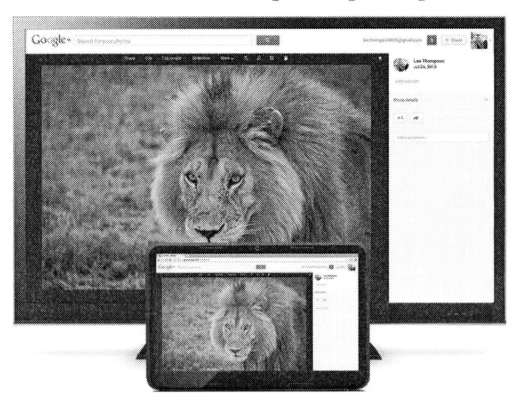

Install Google Cast Extension on your Chrome browser to continue casting Web Pages using Chrome.

Follow the steps below to install Google Cast Extension:

First of all, make sure your Chrome browser is upgraded to the latest version. To ensure, go to Settings and click on the 'About Google Chrome' option. If you are using an old version, upgrade to the latest one now.

Go to Chrome Apps and download Google Cast Extension.

Follow the installation procedure. Once the app is installed, a tiny 'Cast Button' will appear on the top right side of your browser.

Please remember, if your device is already set up, you may not need to install the app again. However, you must download Google Chrome Cast Extension to continue with the procedure.

Now that your Chrome Cast Extension has been installed, you need to follow a few simple steps to be able to use your Chrome browser and web pages using your Chromecast device.

When complete, you will be able to access web pages and play videos directly on your television from casted optimized sites like Netflix.com and YouTube.com. Doing so will also help you cast your browser tab (discussed later in the book).

Here are the steps to follow:

1. Again, make sure you are using the updated version of Chrome browser. If not, update immediately.
2. As you have already downloaded and installed Cast Extension, you will see a tiny cast icon in the toolbar placed at the top right.
3. To cast a tab to your smart Chromecast device to play a show or video directly on your TV, review 'minimum system requirements' to ensure your network and computer are eligible for supporting it.

Congratulations! You are done and ready to get started.

Chromecast Device and Casting an Entire Tab Using Chrome

Once your Chromecast is connected with Chrome, casting a tab is a step away. Follow the steps to begin casting a tab of your browser:

1. You should be on the tab that you wish to project directly on your TV.
2. Next, tap on the Cast Button located at the top right side in the toolbar of your browser.
3. You will see a list of Chromecast devices pop up on your television screen. Pick any device to cast the tab you want to project to this device.
4. The device will take its brief load time after which the current tab will be displayed on your TV.

The Cast icon will change color to signify that it is activated for use and the tab that's projected on your TV screen will automatically glow to indicate it's active.

If you are already using your Chromecast – for instance, it could be playing a video on Netflix or YouTube – when you choose the device or open the menu, you can access a short description of what Chromecast is doing currently. You might also be able to use some controls such as mute, pause etc, for that particular activity.

Tap on the 'Cast this Tab' button to terminate the activity running and cast the tab. This way, you will be sure that you are picking the right device.

You can easily cast significant web content through this procedure. However, websites that require plug-ins such as VLC, Quicktime and Silverlight are not compatible and thus may result in lack of sound or picture.

During the tab casting procedure, images and videos for the casted tab can be viewed on your TV as well as on your computer. However, the output for sound will only be through your TV for the selected tab. Other than the selected tab, other application and tabs will continue to play the sound on your computer. It is possible to switch to other applications or tabs during the tab casting procedure. This is even possible with full-screen mode if you use the Alt+Tab shortcut on the keyboard. For Mac, use the Command Tab.

During the casting procedure, you can tab or click on the small Cast icon again if you wish to take any of the actions mentioned below:

1. Select the status area that displays what tab is being cast currently to return to the first tab you begin casting from.
2. Use the button to mute the video or sound playing on your TV. However, this is distinct depending on the mute function of your TV, so you can unmute from the Chrome browser.
3. Use the Cast icon to stop casting the tab using the 'Stop' button.
4. Closing the tab will also result in stopping the casting process.

Casting Full-Screen Mode

Chromecast is designed to work with certain apps and websites such as Netflix and YouTube. When you watch a video using any of these compatible apps and sites, you can automatically view full screen mode on the cast destination device.

On the other hand, if you are using an unsupported app or site, casting will only display what you are actually viewing on the screen. That is, if you are not watching it on a full screen on your Chrome browser or tab, it won't appear on a full screen mode on the TV you are casting to using your Chromecast device.

However, with a little trick, you can enhance your experience and enlarge the screen as large as a full-screen mode and enjoy. To do so, you can zoom in the site or app using the '+' button on the keyboard or CTRL+ mouse wheel. Once the video gets as large as to fit the entire screen, you can cast it.

The best part is that the zoom setting on your gadget will be carried forward to your TV as well, where you can enjoy a full-screen mode without really using the command. This will also enable you to view other content and switch tabs while casting a video directly to your TV using Chromecast.

Playing Hard Drive Entertainment Files

 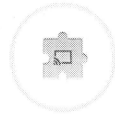  

If you think watching movies or videos right from your hard drive is something you cannot do using Chromecast, you are wrong.

To do so, you first need to check for two settings on your Chrome browser.

Once you have your extension on the right top side of your screen, click and go to options.

The first thing to check in Options is Audio Resizing. Make sure the option is checked.

Next, check Tab Projection Quality and select High (720p) to experience a golden casting.

Next, convert an entertainment piece on your hard drive that you wish to enjoy. Just drag the blue ray on the browser and instantly you will see a black screen, which means it will be working perfectly fine.

Soon you will see the video playing on your Chrome Browser. It is important to know that your file to work fine it should be in an mp4 format or if you files are in mkv files they should be with audio recording with aac.

Let the video play and go back to the casting extension on top right side of your toolbar. Click the Chrome Home option in the drop down menu. Within a few seconds you will have your TV screen showing you the same video in a full-screen mode.

Enjoy your video and repeat to watch any other video you like.

Plex Casting for Free

In addition to YouTube and Netflix, Plex is among the first few apps that has closely worked with Google and has managed to make Chromecast all the more worthwhile.

The most interesting part of adding Plex to Chromecast support is its integration with its existing support for remote control and remote players. The collaboration was made to ensure that user experience across AirPlay devices (iOS), Plex players and Chromecast devices becomes rich and seamless. This also enhanced the remote control support of plex during the process.

Users can now enjoy a better experience when flinging media or controlling all players through remote control, including web player, Android, iOS, Windows 8, the Roku and of course Plex Home Theatre.

Indeed, the platform of Chromecast is superb; a small device is used to run and control the Chrome browser automaticall. As far as plex players are considered, you need to ensure you have the most updated media server installed to make the most out of your Chromecast and Plex casting for free.

And in case you have an android, make sure you install the latest Plex for PlexPass.

23

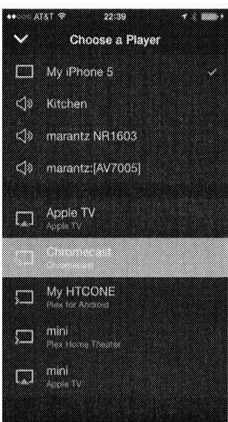

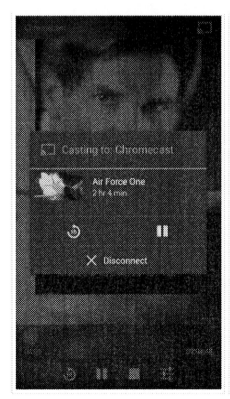

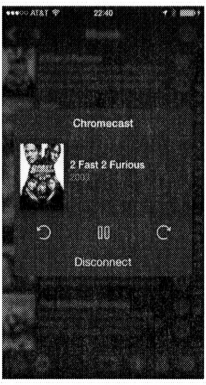

Casting Online – How Chromecast Can Use Grooveshark, Spotify and Media from Your Playlist

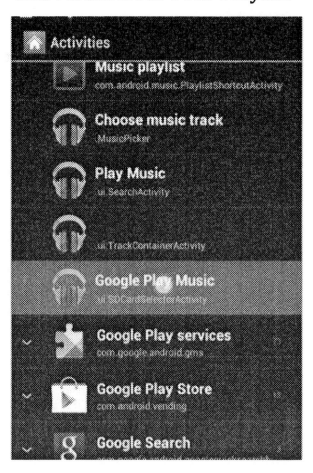

In order to use Grooveshark and Spotify to listen to music through Chromecast, you need to connect with the Google Play App. Once you have casted the Google Play app, you can access Grooveshard and Spotify to listen to music from your play list. This is further explained in detail below.

In order to run Google Play Music app, your Chromecast requires app version 5.0.11 or higher for android. For iOS, Google Play Music App version 1.1.0.988 is ideal. Make sure you update your applications to the latest version to ensure it is compatible with Chromecast.

This smart 2-inch dongle can cast songs from Grooveshark, Spotify using Google Play Music application as well as can play media from your iOS phone, Android phone or

Android tablet. Connect with your TV using the Chromecast device and get grooving with the music of your choice.

Download Google Play music app on your device and purchase songs for your playlist.

To proceed with the casting, follow the steps below:

1. Access Google Play Music application and choose the playlist or song you wish to play.
2. Click on the Cast button located on the top right side of the application. Tap and choose your Chromecast device from the list.
3. Your TV will display a notification that your device is making a secure connection with your Chromecast device and the music will play on your TV in no time.

While your music is playing on your television through Chromecast using your phone or tablet, you can continue using your device to perform other tasks. Your device will no longer be connected to the application and you battery will not drain.

Once your device is connected with your TV through Chromecast, your smart device becomes a remote control for your TV. To do so, chose the Cast button from the notification bar on the top of your device.

To disconnect the connection with Chromecast, tap on the Cast button again and select your device.

A few things to note:

1. Google Play Music application for Chromecast is only available for your iOS or Android tablet or phone, your desktop computer as well as you laptop.

2. Make sure you are using the updated version of the Google Play Music application. If not, please download the update to use Chromecast effectively.

3. Turn on the Wi-Fi on your device and make sure it is connected to the same internet network as your Chromecast device.

4. Google Play Music will not play downloaded or local content saved in your device through Chromecast.

5. Using the application, access Spotify and Grooveshark to listen to free music tracks on your PC or smart device at any time.

6. In case your device lose connection from the network or the battery of your device runs out, the playlist will stop once the current song finishes playing.

Connecting Chromecast with Kindle Fire – How to Cast Music and Instant Video from Amazon Kindle Fire

Good news! Chromecast can be used with Kindle Fire device too. Kindle Fire, which is also considered an Android, is an ideal device to be paired with Chromecast. This is what you need to do:

Step 1: Download a third party application for your Kindle Fire.

Step 2: Go to Play Store and download 1mobilemarket application and install it on your smart kindle device.

Step 3: Access the application and look for play movies, chromecast, play music and YouTube. Install each one of these.

Step 4: When you are done with the installation of the applications, open the Chromecast app on your device and connect it with your device using the same procedures mentioned above.

Step 5: Access media files that you wish to see on your TV and enjoy.

Kindle Fire, a device that offers various entertainments on its own can now be connected with your TV for more fun.

Enjoy your experience of syncing your Kindle Fire device for projecting and broadcasting videos and music on your TV.

Phone or Remote? How Your Android and iOS Can Control Chromecast

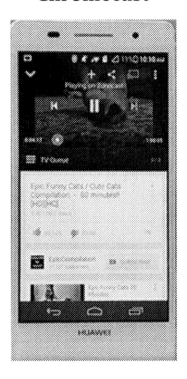

Now that you have connected your TV with your Android or iOS device, your device automatically turns into a remote.

The procedure is so convenient and you can control your TV screen without using its actual remote. Once you sync your device with the TV using Chromecast, your device is free to be used.

The following are some common features that make you use your android or iOS device like a remote control. Read on:

1. Use your android or iOS to pause the video or song.
2. Use your android or iOS to play the video or song.
3. The 10-second replay button will rewind the song or video ten seconds back.
4. You can tap on the stop button on your device to stop the video or song and disconnect the sync immediately.
5. The android or iOS device can also be used to control the volume.

6. Check in for additional settings and enlarging the screen to fit the TV size using your Android or iOS device.

7. Drag the video or audio from one point to another with your smart android or iOS remote.

Chromecast has made world a better place to live in.

Tuning Wireless Video Setting for Chromecast

While the diminutive streamer of Google may not be as friendly for developers as we would have appreciated, official support from content providers and large developers is sure to grow in due time.

In order to enhance your Chromecast broadcasting experience, you need to ensure you have the best internet network to work with. Your local network connection can make a huge difference to ensure your Chromecast dongle works for you. However, the best part is that you still have a few options to configure in the Google Chromcast Plugin to optimize your chromecasting experience.

To work with these plugins, you need to fine tune your tab streaming parameters using Chromecast. By removing display and inspect element, you can access a variety of fine tuning options to optimize your tab sharing experience.

The options available to you include maximum and minimum video bit rate, maximum frames per second, quantization, debugging options and audio bitrate.

Make Chromecast Mobile with Travel Router

While your little dongle can travel with you wherever you like, taking along a travel router can make things so much easier.

With a travel router in hand, you can connect and enjoy casting anywhere in the world, where you have internet, a smart device and of course, a large TV.

If you are traveling to a different city or country and planning to stay in a hotel, make the most out of the internet facility available. Just connect the internet with your portable travel router and get started immediately.

Plug in your Chromecast device to your TV in the same way mentioned above and connect your device and chromecast to the internet service available and you are free to watch videos and listen to music using your device as a remote control.

So a few more bucks for an additional investment on a travel router and you will never get bored on a vacation at home.

You have some of the tiniest routers available that will not take much space in your luggage. These palm size routers are quite affordable and can make the entire vacation and traveling much more fun.

Get your hands on your travel router now!

Charismatic Chrome for a Yell-Out YouTube Party

A party with a little dongle?

Sounds weird but now that you own a Google Chromecast, it is definitely possible.

Connect your little device with your TV and play music and music videos without the costly DJ setup.

You have no idea how loud your little Chromecast dongle can get.

Just connect Chromecast with your TV and control the volume either with the TV's remote control or by using your device as the remote control.

The volume of your TV will analyze how successful your YouTube party will be.

Sync and access YouTube and play music videos on your TV. Adjust volume accordingly and enjoy every bit of it.

If you want to follow the dance moves, the screen is right in front of you. Follow the steps and impress people with your skills as well as you little dongle device.

For people who can't move on the dance floor will still be able to enjoy the party as there will be a larger screen playing the best of video songs.

Remember to create a playlist on YouTube beforehand and let it play all night!

An important thing to note:

As you know that your casting requires a solid internet connection, make sure you have a good backup to avoid spoiling your party at the last minute because of a crappy connection.

The Idea behind Using Chromecast Abroad

Carrying your Chromecast device and travel router with you has more advantages than you can think. Traveling to a different country means watching their local channels that could be in different languages.

Don't leave your entertainment gadget with you back home when traveling abroad. The idea behind making Chromecast so mobile is to let you carry your entertainment with you wherever you go.

Get a nice internet connection and sync your device with the television and access several applications and channels that are compatible with your Chromecast. Unlike before, now you have a long list of apps and channels that you can use with your Chromecast.

Access your favorite channel or use your favorite app and enjoy a large display on a TV.

Getting to Know More about Chromecast's Advanced Settings

Discovering more about Chromecast and getting to know its advanced settings can significantly improve your chrome experience. The following are some tips and tricks to follow.

1. **Play local files from your PC**

You may not have an idea but it is possible to stream local content stored on your computer using your Chromecast device. Sync the TV with your computer and access the Chrome browser.

Click on the File menu and choose Open File option on the list. Next, chose the file you would like to broadcast on your TV.

The file saved on your computer will open in a new browser tab. You can use this link to cast to your television with the help of Chromecast browser extension you can see in the top right side of your screen.

2. Tune Settings to Enhance Video Playback

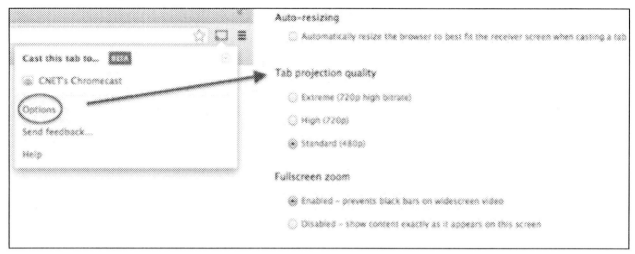

As we all know, Chromecast is greatly dependant on a strong and stready Wi-Fi connection for streaming. If the videos you play have a choppy playback or is constantly suffering from buffering interruptions, it is highly recommended that you tune and reduce your settings for video playback.

To do so, access the Chromecast options located on the top right side of your Chrome browser. Tap or click on the tiny icon and select Options. Under Tab Projection Quality, select Standard (480p). With an insignificant hit in the video quality, you can enjoy better playback quality with little or no interruptions at all.

Refer to the image above to follow the options for settings.

3. Access Hidden Chromecast Settings

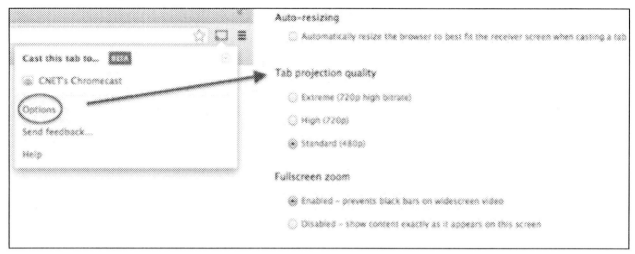

There's a hidden settings menu for Chromecast that advanced users may want to explore. These settings can help you adjust the frame rate, maximum bit rate, minimum bit rate and other useful things. If this sounds unfamiliar, you can skip this step (targeted towards advanced users only)

In the extension options of the Chromecast browser, right click and select the Inspect Element option from the list. Search for the line that contains the text "quality == custom," and expand your selection. Delete where it says "Display; none."

Scroll down and you will see the same text again. Delete where it says "Display; none" again and close the box. The hidden setting menu will appear.

While some users share their experience of improved streaming after the settings were altered, others believe that they the advanced setting menu may not be active as yet.

Google Cast extension options

Custom mirroring settings

Changing these may have unintended consequences. Be careful.

Video Settings

Minimum bitrate: [   ] kbps (min)

Maximum bitrate: [   ] kbps (max)

Max quantization: [   ]

Video buffer: [   ] ms

Maximum tab frame rate: [   ] fps

Resolution:

Audio Settings

Audio bitrate: [   ] kbps (-)

Network Settings

Pacing: ○ Enable pacing (M28 or later)

TCP: ○ Enable audio TCP ○ Enable video TCP

NACK: ○ Enable Audio NACK

4. Use Your Device While Streaming Videos with Chromecast

When using a smart device for chromecasting, you can easily multitask and use your device for other functions while streaming videos and audios.

On the other hand, if you are chromecasting from your computer's or laptop's web browser, you are forced to keep the video in full screen mode and utilizing your computer or laptop only for a single, chromecasting task.

The good news is that you can fix this. While streaming a full-screen video on your TV using your computer, hit Alt+Tab on windows and choose the desktop. This will enable you to perform multiple tasks on your computer while streaming the video through Chromecast.

For OS X, you can use the Command+Tab, select Finder,follow the Chrome icon on your dock. Right click and chose Hide from the list. This way you can perform other tasks while streaming, effectively.

5. Mirroring Computer's Display on Television

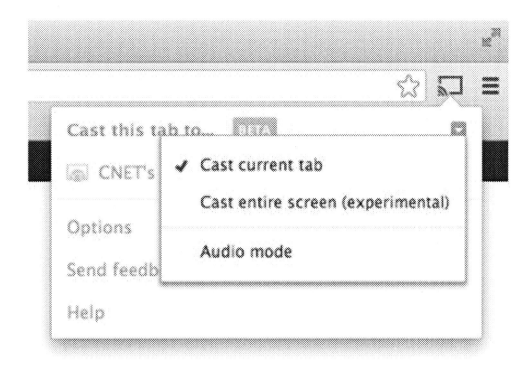

Indeed, Chromecast is designed to stream videos and audio from your smart device and/or computer to your TV. It is also capable of casting a tab from the web browser. However, did you know you can mirror the entire desktop of your computer through Chromecast? Yes you can!

To do so, open the Chromecast extension available on the top right side of the browser. Check out the first option that says, 'Cast this tab to…'. Click on the tiny drop down menu button to see further options. Select the second option that says, 'Cast entire screen'. By clicking on the option, you can view your computer's desktop on your TV.

Note here that this option is regarded as Experimental by Google, which is a warning that this option may not work perfectly and may even crash frequently. Also note that this option does not sync the playback of your computer with your TV and you will still hear the sound coming from your computer's speakers and not the TV.

Factory Settings can be Reset, Learn How

There may come a point when you wish to reset your Chromecast back to factory settings either to get over with any problem you have been facing or to erase the name you have given to the device or even if you wish to change the network you have been using previously.

First of all, you need to know that there are two ways to reset your device. First, you can do it using the Chromecast app by finding the Reset to Factory Settings option under Settings or Menu.

Another and more popular way to reset is to do it physically using the reset button on the Chromecast device.

Follow the steps below to reset your device back to factory settings through the physical method.

1. Find the reset button located right next to the charging slot on the Chromecast device.

2. Next, plug the Device into your TV and wait till the light turns on.

3. When the device is connected with your TV, press and hold the reset button for at least 25-30 seconds to activate the reset option.

4. The screen will cut itself off the moment your reset option is activated. The light on your Chromecast device will also change to red.

5. Soon you will see your screen appear again as the Chromecast is loading to set up. This is your reset mode.

6. Your Chromecast device is now back to its default factory settings, meaning it has erased the name you have given it earlier as well as the wireless network.

7. Your device is now just like brand new. You will be taken back to the Set Me Up page where you will need to input the device name and network again.

Follow the same procedure to set up the device mentioned above.

The screen above is what you will see after resetting back to the factory settings.

Taking Your Chromecast Device One Step Ahead

Google Chrome has introduced a new and creative method for broadcasting that enables the user to pull in the demanded media directly from the Internet.

With more and more users of Chromecast, the usability has evolved beyond expectations. Also, with a large number of applications that are available for this service now, the user experience has enhanced tremendously.

In the beginning, the Chromecast worked only with a small group of services or starters mentioned below:

1. YouTube – website and mobile application
2. Netflix – website and mobile application
3. Google Play Music – mobile application for Android only
4. Google Play Movies and TV –mobile application for Android only

Applications for Chromecast

The following is the current list of applications that can be used with Chromecast for enhanced usability. More apps are made to take user experience with Chromecast to the next level.

Check out each of these applications in detail below:

1. Netflix

Stream Netflix on your large TV screen and watch thousands of movies, TV shows and Netflix original programming on your television screen using Chromecast.

2. YouTube

Go big with this amazing device letting you stream your favorite videos and music on your large TV screen. The best YouTube channels can now be accessed with your TV with the smart Chromecast Google device.

3. Red Bull TV

Red Bull TV offers inspiration programming that can now be enjoyed on the best screen in your house. Enjoy the extensive selection of lifestyle entertainment, music and sports on your TV screen by casting it through Chromecast.

4. Hulu Plus

Enjoy the best and most popular TV shows by streaming Hulu Plus application through Chromecast. Sync your device with your Television and make the most out of your Hulu Plus subscription.

5. HBO GO

The original series of HBO Go as well the most popular and hit movies are just a click away if you have Chromecast and HBO Go app. Connect and watch your favorite shows on your TV now.

6. Pandora

Take your little radio to the large screen by using the Pandora app with your Chromecast. Listen to personalized, free radio with this great app on the large speakers of your television. Enjoy!

7. Google Play Music

Listen to the rocking millions of your favorite songs on the best speakers of your house. Connect your Chromecast with your TV and sync with this amazing app. Your new dance floor is now right in the middle of your living room with this amazing Google Play Music application.

8. Google Play TV and Movies

The best collection of movies and TV shows are now a click away with this amazing application, which is now available for Chromecast. Google Play TV and Movies is all that you want to make the most out of your Chromecasting experience.

Why You Need a Chromecast

You definitely need Chromecast because this isn't all. There is more streaming in soon to make your Chromecast experience a lifetime experience.

This book reveals all that you need to know about Chromecast and things that are not revealed here are left for you to experience yourself.

Grab your $35 dongle now and experience what real entertainment is all about.

Your TV was never this worthy before!

So get started and enjoy every minute of your Chromecast device ownership!